Abstract

Providing for the Common Defense…Within our Borders

This book examines U.S. law regarding use of the U.S. Armed Forces in domestic affairs. A brief scenario involving a terrorist attack using a weapon of mass destruction introduces an example of the dangers inherent in the use of military forces to regain or maintain public law and order. The discussion of U.S. law begins with the history of Posse Comitatus and proceeds through the passage of the Homeland Security Act of 2002. The Department of Homeland Security was created by this law and a subsequent action of establishing a unified commander with geographic responsibilities for the North American continent have been questioned as a breach of this law and a threat to civil liberties of American citizens.

Upon examination of written law of the land and U.S. tradition, missions and functions of USNORTHCOM are consistent with U.S law and the constitutional duty of the federal government. Despite compliance with the law, involvement of military forces within our borders is contrary to U.S. tradition raising public concerns with the application and involvement of military forces. Concerns for USNORTHCOM are addressed at the operational and national-strategic level regarding the interaction of military forces with the civilian population and public relations. Public perception driven by operations conducted within our borders will be a serious and continuing public relations challenge unique to the Commander of USNORTHCOM.

INTRODUCTION

It is a hot summer day in New England and tourists are quickly vacating the streets to make the nightly curfew. Life has been tough in these small New England towns that were once thriving hubs of tourism. Local economic depression brought on by the 10:00 PM curfew, restricted airline travel and soaring gas prices have greatly impacted the cash flow from tourism once considered the life's blood of this small town. Many restaurants and bars dependent on tourism are slowly vanishing from the landscape under the greatly reduced flow of vacationers. The corresponding loss of summer jobs and annual income is showing in the mood and attitude of the population. Poverty is on the rise and the crime rate is seeing upward pressure from public desperation and the strict imposition of tougher laws strictly enforced by military troops. The fabric of civil society in the country seems to be unraveling under the stress brought about by the war on terrorism. A once free and thriving populace now cowers with insecurity and the frustration grows, as security measures perceived to be ineffective, have restricted personal freedoms. Lost personal freedom has degraded the pursuit of life, liberty and happiness, but has not resulted in an assurance of security in the lives of the populace. Many public officials now understand how this new trend in American life began but none have a reasonable solution to reverse the problem of lost freedoms. A proper solution would serve to restore confidence, prosperity and liberties while striking a balance between public security and personal freedoms.

July 20, 2007 is a date most Americans now have seared into their memories. This was the date of the attack two years ago causing the President to order military troops into Boston on a mission of pacification after the so-called "Boston Bombing." This terrorist event rivaled the more infamous tragedies in American history and shares a death toll similar to the World Trade Center on 9/11. It also holds a public shock value equivalent to that of the Oklahoma City bombing of 1995 but the similarity stops there. Public anger and fear peaked in the aftermath of the 2007 "Boston Bombing" because military troops were used to suppress the unrest and looting. The dozens killed in the attempt to restore order surpassed the emotional trauma felt from the blast of the terrorist's weapon. When an angry, lawless mob turned on the soldiers, their self-defense measures resulted in dozens of deaths from automatic weapons fire. Not unlike the Boston Massacre of 1775, the truth was obscured in press reports and public distrust was inflamed beyond the boiling point.[1]

The genesis of these events was a terrorist attack in which a dirty nuclear weapon was detonated near the U.S.S. Constitution in downtown Boston. Despite the best efforts of the U.S. Government, coordinated through the Department of Homeland Security and implemented by United States Northern Command (USNORTHCOM), the terrorist attack proved deadly to thousands in the Boston area. Terrorists, for population density and symbolic value, selected this site to further their twisted objective. To plant fear into the nation by creating a significant loss of life, destroy a valued American landmark, the U.S.S. Constitution and undermine the strength of the nation by attacking the principles underpinning our government, the U.S. Constitution. Strong winds carried radioactive debris as far as East Boston and fortunately carried the preponderance of the debris across the river keeping the downtown area relatively free from the effects. The chaos and looting in the aftermath of the disaster resulted in the eventual mobilization of military forces, under command of USNORTHCOM, to establish law and order, but the chaos quickly spread along the eastern seaboard from Rhode Island to Maine as inaccurate press reports of the "Second Boston Massacre" were published.

---

[1] David McCullough, John Adams (Simon & Schuster, 2001), 65-66.

Escalation of terrorist activities has been the recent trend and a terrorist event such as this has been feared and forecast since the early 1990's.[2] Numerous laws, Presidential Decision Directives and government reorganizations have been made over the past decade in an attempt to prevent this tragedy, and in the worst case, if prevention failed, deal with the aftermath.[3] Laws passed in the 1990's brought the expertise of the U.S. military into the realm of available resources in the event of a nuclear, chemical or biological weapon was used against the population. The reorganization of the military in 2002 established USNORTHCOM, a military command to provide this assistance.[4] Where was the point of no return on the slippery slope of military involvement in civil affairs? Perhaps the events leading to our "Second Boston Massacre" and necessitating a long term Army presence in the area was merely the symptom of forgotten historical lessons or was this simply blatant violation of U.S. law?

The use of the U.S. military forces for missions within the borders of our country has historically been a matter of contention.[5] U.S. law bounds military actions but many units are not aware of legal constraints nor do they train to conduct operations within our borders with an emphasis on preserving civil liberties. The recent establishment of a combatant commander with responsibilities over the continental United States in cooperation with the Department of Homeland Security brings new challenges in mission, implementation and public relations. This paper will cover the origins of Posse Comitatus and subsequent amendments leading to the present day. It will also briefly examine the vast reorganization

---

[2] Judith L. Gentner, "The American Dilemma: Freedoms or Security." (Unpublished Research Paper, U.S. Army War College, Carlisle Barracks, PA: 1999), 7.

[3] General Military Law, U. S. Code Title 10, Section 381, (1981). Also derived from Presidential Decision Directive 63 and Homeland Security Act of 2002.

[4] U.S. Department of Defense. Unified Command Plan. (Washington, DC: April 2002), 10.

[5] David E. Engdahl, "Foundations for the Military Intervention in the United States." In Military Intervention in Democratic Societies, ed. Peter J. Rowe and Christopher J. Whelan, (London: Croom Helm, 1985), 25.

of the federal government resulting from the war on terrorism and establishment of a

combatant commander with responsibility to matters inside the geographic bounds of the

continental United States. In conclusion, it will discuss the legal implications of the unique

and groundbreaking challenges to USNORTHCOM with respect to the mission and

implications of public perception of those actions.

U.S. LAW and POSSE COMITATUS

The traditions opposing the use of military forces in the enforcement of civilian law

in this country precede the country's foundation.[6] Roots extending into England's history

and law shaped the writers thoughts while drafting the U.S. Constitution. The colonial

experience with the British military was another shaping force as the colonies began the

quest for self-rule. The use of British troops during the period leading up to and including

the American Revolution led to this being a primary grievance written into the Declaration of

Independence. Also, ratification of the U.S. Constitution met opposition from many states on

the grounds congressional oversight and civilian control placed over standing armies were

insufficient to prevent military intervention in domestic civil affairs. No direct prohibition on

military involvement in civil law enforcement made the final draft of the constitution, but the

language Madison included to settle the debate and gain support for the document was, "No

person shall…be deprived of life, liberty, or property without due process of law."[7]

Posse Comitatus came about, almost one hundred years later, as a result of disputes

over the use of federal troops in the south in the aftermath of the Civil War. Federal troops

had ousted state governors and state legislatures at the conclusion of the Civil War claiming

---

[6] Ibid, 3-8.
[7] U.S. Constitution, Amendment V.

no legal governments were in power and the military troops were there to represent the federal government's authority and enforce the laws.

A second impetus was the usage of troops in the west to subdue Indian populations and any other alleged or real criminals. Fort commanders were the only government entity able to exercise civilian law enforcement and the remote locations justified these actions. Laws were sometimes enforced in arbitrary ways resulting in constitutional violations.[8]

Congress finally acted in response to events surrounding the presidential elections of 1876. Despite post war reconstruction of governments in secessionist states being complete by 1870, the federal troops remained in many states seizing political prisoners, interfering with civil state governments and reconstituting state legislatures.[9] Democratic candidate for President Tilden won the popular vote but the Electoral College votes went to the republican candidate Hayes and this altered the outcome of the election. Congress believed republican governments were being held in power in Louisiana and South Carolina through coercion exerted by the federal troops. President Grant took exception to the premise claiming use of the military was merely "to secure the better execution of the laws of the United States"[10] and this was well within his constitutional duties and an inherent executive power of the presidency. To settle this dispute the Posse Comitatus Act was passed as a rider to the 1880 Army appropriations bill. After an initial veto by President Hayes the act became law on June 18, 1878 and reads as follows:

Chapter 263, Section 15

From and after the passage of this act it shall not be lawful to employ any part of the Army of the United States, as a posse comitatus, or otherwise, for the purpose of executing laws, except in such cases and under such circumstances as such

---

[8] Bonnie Baker, "The Origins of the Posse Comitatus." Aerospace Power Chronicles (November 1999), 1.
[9] Engdahl, 22.
[10] Engdahl, 23.

employment of said force may be expressly authorized by the Constitution or by act of Congress...

Subsequent changes to the laws impacting military involvement in civilian law enforcement were deliberated in 1981 and passed as part of the Defense Department Authorization Act of 1982.[11] The country's war on drugs spawned these changes to aid law enforcement coverage of vast areas of land, sea and air through which the illegal drug trade was operating.[12] Sections 371-378 were added to title 10 of the U.S.C. to clarify the extent of military involvement without violating posse comitatus. Collectively these changes allow the military to provide expertise, training, assistance, information and materiel to civilian law enforcement officials in the performance of their duties. Despite the broad nature of the allowances listed above title 10 U.S.C., section 375 prohibits "direct participation by military personnel." Specifically mentioned in this section, the law does not "permit direct participation by a member of the Army, Navy, Air Force, or Marine Corps in a search, seizure, arrest, or other similar activity unless participation in such activity by such member is otherwise authorized by law."[13]

As the War on Terrorism moved to the forefront on the list of national priorities in the late 1990's further clarification was forthcoming with regard to the coordination and participation of military and civil law enforcement.

> "While speaking at Annapolis in May 1998, President Clinton urged the cooperation of the armed forces with law enforcement, intelligence, and other federal agencies under the coordination of the National Coordinator for Security, Infrastructure Protection and Counterterrorism. In accord with this view, President Clinton's mandates in PDD 63 expressly contemplate cooperation among all government

---

[11] Engdahl, 25.
[12] Gregory D. Grove, The U.S. Military and the Civil Infrastructure Protection: Restrictions and Discretion under the Posse Comitatus Act. (Stanford, CA: Center for International Security and Cooperation, 1999), 22.
[13] General Military Law, U. S. Code Title 10, Section 375, (1981).

agencies including the FBI, DoD, and the intelligence agencies to achieve and maintain critical infrastructure protection."[14]

These were changes brought in the aftermath of the of 1993 World Trade Center bombing and the 1995 Oklahoma City Bombing in an attempt to bring all the nation's resources to bare against the threat of terrorism.

As the terrorist threat continues growing toward the use of weapons of mass destruction changes to U.S. law were made to clarify use of military resources. For example, the National Defense Authorization Act of 1997 required the Secretary of Defense to provide training and advice in situations of crisis involving biological and chemical weapons of mass destruction while emphasizing the restrictions delineated in title 10, U.S.C. section 375 regarding a prohibition on direct action of military members involving search and seizure.[15] A similar law regarding the offenses related to the use of nuclear weapons is addressed in title 18, U.S.C. section 831. A primary difference in this law is the allowance of searches and seizures conducted by Department of Defense personnel when the offense is related to nuclear materials.[16]

Since the events of 9/11 the coordination between federal agencies has been codified through changes in the laws and government reorganization. The USA Patriot Act of 2001 began the emphasis on changing the legal landscape to enhance the nation's security. A primary purpose of this law was "to deter and punish terrorist acts in the United States and around the world, to enhance law enforcement investigatory tools, and for other purposes."[17]

---

[14] Grove, 27.

[15] Nolon J. Benson, The Posse Comitatus Act: Is There a Need for Change?, (Unpublished Research Paper, Carlisle Barrack, PA: U.S. Army War College, 1998), 8.

[16] U.S.Code Title 18, Section 831, (1982): "...use of personnel of the Department of Defense to arrest persons and conduct searches and seizures with respect to violations of this section; and such other activity as is incidental to the enforcement of this section, or to the protection of persons or property from conduct that violates this section."

[17] Public Law 107-56, USA Patriot Act, (2001).

The subsequent move to enhance national security against terrorism and further define the coordination between government agencies began with PDD 63 has evolved into a government reorganization undertaken by the Homeland Security Act of 2002. This new organizational structure will be the mechanism to deter and defend the nation against further terrorist attack and a new combatant commander, with responsibilities within the continental U.S., will direct and coordinate the military involvement.

The extent military personnel will become involved in future law enforcement matters, as the war of terrorism progresses is as unpredictable as the circumstances surrounding the next major war. Environments of uncertainty typical of military operations persist on this new frontier of combating terrorists. In regards to constitutionality of military troops being used to enforce civil law it is more a matter of tradition and implication rather than strict letter of the constitution. Further laws were passed in the Civil War era codifying the tradition of civil law enforcement being kept out of military auspices. This law expressly forbids the use of the U.S. Army to enforce civil law. The Department of the Navy adheres to this as a matter of policy.[18] These laws, prior to any amendments, allowed for military participation in execution of civil law enforcement when authorized by congress or the constitution, but the recent trend continues to bring a more active role to military forces with respect to civil law enforcement. More recent changes to title 10 clarify the limitations of posse comitatus and give substantial latitude for government officials needing military assistance in training personnel and materiel, but the most rigid prohibitions, those of search, seizure and arrest, are removed in the event of nuclear threats to the nation. Therefore, USNORTHCOM has very wide latitude in operations within the designated area of responsibility. Any action taken in support of civilian officials or agencies will *not* violate the letter of the constitution and *with* congressional authorization the military's resources could be fully incorporated into operations of civil law enforcement without violating U.S. law. This was addressed in great detail in the Homeland Security Act of 2002:

> "Congress finds the following: …The Posse Comitatus Act has served the Nation well in limiting the use of the Armed Forces to enforce the law. Nevertheless, by its express terms, the Posse Comitatus Act is not a complete barrier to the use of the Armed Forces for a range of domestic purposes, including law enforcement functions, when the use of the Armed Forces is authorized by Act of Congress or the President determines that the use of the Armed Forces is required to fulfill the President's obligations under the Constitution to respond promptly in time of war, insurrection, or other serious emergency…Congress reaffirms the continued importance of section 1385 of title 18, United States Code, and it is the sense of Congress that nothing in this Act should be construed to alter the applicability of such section to any use of the Armed Forces as a posse comitatus to execute the laws."[19]

DEPARTMENT OF HOMELAND SECURITY

The vision for a Department of Homeland Security was published in July 2002 in the National Strategy for Homeland Security. This document was published prior to passage of legislation creating the Department of Homeland Security and sets three strategic objectives for the new department. These objectives are preventing terrorist attacks within our borders, reducing vulnerability to terrorist attacks and minimize the damage from attacks that may occur. Departmental functions are listed as "six critical mission areas: intelligence and warning, border and transportation security, domestic counter-terrorism, protecting critical infrastructure and key assets, defending against catastrophic terrorism, and emergency preparedness and response. The first three mission areas focus primarily on preventing terrorist attacks; the next two on reducing our Nation's vulnerabilities; and the final one on minimizing the damage and recovering from attacks that do occur."[20]

---

[18] Grove, 14.

[19] Public Law 107-296, Homeland Security Act of 2002, (2002).

[20] Office of Homeland Security. National Strategy for Homeland Security. (Washington, DC: July 2002), viii.

The Homeland Security Act of 2002 established the department as a focal point for coordination among government agencies and other entities possessing resources critical to the deterrence, defense or reaction to terrorist events. Despite this focus the department does not hold primary responsibility for investigating or prosecuting violations of the law regarding terrorism. This function is left to the jurisdiction of the various federal, state and local law enforcement agencies except those transferred to the department.[21]

The Secretary of Homeland Security is authorized to "attend and participate" in meetings of the National Security Council at the discretion of the President.[22] A separate Homeland Security Council is established consisting of the President, Vice President, Secretary of Homeland Security, Attorney General, Secretary of Defense and any other designated by the President to provide advice on matters relating to homeland security.[23] The Secretary's authority does not extend to the conduct of military activities including war fighting and military defense of the country and the reorganization under this act does not change the authority of the Secretary of Defense.[24]

A final significant point regarding the law establishing this department is direction to the Secretary of Homeland Security regarding authority to establish a Joint Task Force. The law states he may establish and operate a Joint Interagency Homeland Security Task Force comprised of military and civilian representatives from government agencies to augment the mission of the department.[25] As an example, the law lists the Joint Interagency Task Forces used in Key West, FL. and Alameda, CA. for drug interdiction operations.

---

[21] Public Law 107-296, Homeland Security Act of 2002, Section 101, (2002).
[22] Ibid, section 102d.
[23] Ibid, section 901.
[24] Ibid, section 876.
[25] Ibid, section 885.

UNITED STATES NORTHERN COMMAND

In response to the increased emphasis on Homeland Security within the National Security Strategy the Secretary of Defense has reorganized the Unified Combatant Commands to provide a combatant commander with a geographic area of responsibility over the continental United States and North America. Primary responsibilities include providing assistance to U.S. civil authorities for numerous functions.[26] This command will be the primary provider of military assistance to the Department of Homeland Security. The mission for this command is stated as "homeland defense and civil support, specifically:

- Conduct operations to deter, prevent, and defeat threats and aggression aimed at the United States, its territories, and interests within the assigned area of responsibility; and

- As directed by the President or Secretary of Defense, provide military assistance to civil authorities including consequence management operations."[27]

Few forces are permanently assigned to USNORTHCOM and U.S. Joint Forces Command will provide any additional forces required for operations. Three subordinate Joint Task Forces will conduct ongoing routine operations. JTF Headquarters Homeland Security is responsible for maritime defense planning and assistance to civil authorities. JTF Civil Support handles command and control consequence management in response to events dealing with chemical, biological, radiological, nuclear and high-yield explosives. Joint Task Force 6 supports law enforcement agencies in the area of counter-drug operations. The greatest attribute to the change is a unity of command brought into the efforts to combat terrorism and respond to catastrophic events, whether natural disasters or terrorist attack.

---

[26] U.S. Department of Defense. Unified Command Plan. (Washington, DC: April 2002).
[27] "Who We Are-Mission." USNORTHCOM webpage. <http://www.northcom.mil>, [28 March 2003].

RECOMMENDATIONS

The following recommendations are directed to the USNORTHCOM staff for planning consideration. These recommendations are pertinent to operational concerns dealing with the interaction between military forces and the civilian populace. Additional concerns are stated later for consideration by the Commander of USNORTHCOM in dealing with public relations and will impact the command and country at the national-strategic level.

The opening scenario for this paper depicted a situation similar to the use of military forces to suppress the 1992 Los Angeles riots. Missions such as this bring the differences of civilian law enforcement training and military training to the forefront. Protection of civil liberties and the use of deadly force are two stark contrasts. Civil law enforcement emphasizes the protection of civil rights while the military trains like it fights under the expectation it will eventually fight the way it has trained. For the military using deadly force is a primary method of subduing an enemy and crushing the enemy's will to resist. In law enforcement deadly force is used only to protect human life, either in self-defense, the lives of others involved or innocent bystanders.[28]

Liability for harm or injury caused by the misapplication of military force to the civilian populace is an area not fully resolved by the courts. Historically military members found in the line of duty are not liable for damage or injury caused by their actions. Much of this comes from the member being in a situation dictated by following orders and actions taken are not a result of a personal plan or choice. This supports the efficiency of action greatly needed in a military organization to support an aggressive war fighting mentality. If a question of liability were to enter into the soldiers' mind the decisive actions needed in

---

[28] Kurt Andrew Schlichter, "Locked and Loaded: Taking Aim at the Growing Use of the American Military in Civilian Law Enforcement Operations," (Loyola of Los Angeles Law Review, Summer 1993).

combat would dull the fighting spirit, morale, retention and impede recruiting. If this were changed and civil liability applied to military members the limited personal assets of most military personnel to resolve personal claims would likely be insufficient to justly compensate a grieved party.[29]

Rules of engagement constructed by operational planners should consider the soldier's or marine's training and state of mind entering a crisis situation. When the above concerns of deadly force and lack of liability merge into a single situation, the combination is ripe for an over exertion of force with little or no accountability and this should be a governing factor for the planner. An example of this is highlighted in opening fictional scenario, but unfortunately, American history has myriad examples of such occurrences. An organized staff charged with the responsibility of the homeland must incorporate these lessons into future operations.

Public concern does exist that USNORTHCOM is the beginning step on the path towards a military dictatorship within the U. S.[30] Although not a view held by the majority of the nation, it is a public relations reality which USNORTHCOM must consider and does acknowledge in published information. This view will remain a part of public opinion to a degree directly related with the level of trust citizens hold in their military and government. This opinion will be voiced as long as the first amendment rights remain intact which ironically may depend on how well USNORTHCOM performs its' duties. This is a unique public relations challenge for this command, having responsibility within our borders makes it unique and exacerbates the sensitivity of public opinion and relations. For the commander

---

[29] Kurt Andrew Schlichter, "Locked and Loaded: Taking Aim at the Growing Use of the American Military in Civilian Law Enforcement Operations," (Loyola of Los Angeles Law Review, Summer 1993).
[30] Mark Sonnenblick, Will USNORTHCOM Bring Us Military Dictatorship After Oct 1? Executive Intelligence Weekly, 19 May 2002.

of USNORTHCOM this is a national-strategic level of concern, maintaining the will of the people behind the command's operations in the war on terror is paramount. Despite the overwhelming military strength and resources at the disposal of the U.S. military this war could stumble along the same path of the Vietnam Conflict if public trust is not maintained.

Another crucial element that is being addressed by USNORTHCOM is the necessity of rapid and accurate information flowing to the public in the event of a crisis. The opening scenario referred to inaccurate press reports fueling public distrust labeling an incident of self-defense as the "Second Boston Massacre." This misled an emotionally charged public creating wide spread unrest and rioting after the terrorist attack. Air Force Maj. Gen. Dale Meyerrose, serving as chief information officer for USNORTHCOM recently addressed a homeland security summit in Washington stating "that making the same information available to everyone concerned with a domestic crisis as quickly as possible is critical to homeland security."[31] With suspicions regarding the new unified command being debated in press, government and public forums a misunderstanding or misinterpretation of actual events could prove disastrous leading to events similar to those in the opening scenario. Perhaps a concept of embedded media as used in our most recent conflict should be used by USNORTHCOM to the maximum extent possible in any crisis.

"The idea of having a discrete domestic military command is not new…but it has been opposed by civil libertarians from the political left and right who contend that expanding the military's role in domestic affairs will lead to civil rights abuses."[32] Acknowledging the sensitivities of establishing a military command with responsibilities over the U.S. territory, USNORTHCOM has published internet materials filled with

---

[31] Bob Haskell, "Special to the American Forces Press Service," 26 Nov 2002, <http://www.pentagon.mil/news/Nov2002/n11262002_200211262.html > [4 May 2003].

information regarding Posse Comitatus and serving to clarify the roles and functions of the command. Some of the more significant items are statements that USNORTHCOM "will *not*:

- Create a new agency or military service
- Liaison directly with the Office of Homeland Security or the anticipated Department of Homeland Security. DoD conducts interagency liaison.
- Conduct law enforcement operations
- Secure airports
- Secure borders
- Provide "first responders" (role of federal, state and local community authorities)
- Train and maintain operational forces"[33]

This is an obvious attempt to relieve the concerns of many government officials and citizens that USNORTHCOM will remain within the prescribed mission and not exceed the intended boundaries. Gen Eberhart, Commander of USNORTHCOM, addressed this notion before the House Armed Services Committee in response to "many of the House committee members" expressing concern the operations may endanger the concept of posse comitatus. Eberhart responded stating: "We will remain vigilant in ensuring that USNORTHCOM is used in accordance with the law. We understand the Posse Comitatus Act and related laws…as amended, [it] provides the authority we need to do our job."[34]

CONCLUSION

Military forces are a significant cost to the taxpayers and often looked upon as an under-utilized manpower resource in peacetime. Due to historic successes in time of war and other national crisis our armed forces are respected as effective organizations in solving complex problems. To allow an effective organization with the capability to solve a

---

[32] Dao, James, A Nation Challenged: Domestic Defense, New York Times, 27 Jan 2002, pg A-7.
[33] "Who We Are-Limitations." USNORTHCOM webpage. <http://www.northcom.mil>, [28 March 2003].

particular problem to remain relatively idle in a time of crisis appears wasteful. But using this force distracts from the training that shapes the force into the effective organization it is. Repeated uses outside the bounds of the normal missions cannot occur without fundamentally changing the organization. If the recurring uses are substantially different from the original mission, the distractions erode the high quality training and other characteristics that resulted in the organization being the chosen entity to perform complex tasks. This is a common argument posed in writings refuting the use of military for domestic purposes and does deserve some merit.

A contrary view could be expressed that our world and nation are in a state of constant change and the military services provided yesterday by the nation's military may not fill tomorrow's needs. Defense of our nation has seen a fundamental change since the end of the Cold War. It has changed from deterrence of an enemy alliance believed to be on par, if not superior in certain areas, to defending the nation against small states with militaries less effective than our own. A more recent evolutionary step has been to defend the nation against sub-state actors with a destructive potential serious enough to be a credible threat to a large portion of the populace. If the most significant threat to this nation is a sub-state actor our resources including military manpower, training and force structure should be adjusted accordingly. If defense of the nation requires action within our own borders the federal government is obligated by constitutional duty to take this action. Applying the most effective means available should be the primary concern rather than protecting an obsolete military force structure. Events throughout history surrounding the misuse or abuse of

---

[34] Scott Elliot. "Eberhart Briefs Congress on U.S. Northern Command." NORTHCOM webpage. 14 March 2002. <www.northcom.mil>, [28 March 2003].

military forces in domestic affairs should serve as valued lessons, but not impediments to the future defense of the nation.

As proposed, USNORTHCOM's mission and functions are not in conflict with current laws. The amendments to Posse Comitatus give great latitude in assistance provided to civil law enforcement. Providing expertise, training and equipment have been addressed in current U.S. law and coordination of such activities is the primary reason for the creation of USNORTHCOM. The unity of command will serve other government agencies in the efficient use of military resources most notably surrounding containment and recovery from an incident involving a weapon of mass destruction. Stepping beyond the designed functions in an overzealous manner will be the primary danger of encroaching on civil liberties and numerous prohibited activities are publicly addressed by USNORTHCOM to counter public apprehension.

The oath of office for a military officer reads: "to defend the Constitution of the United States against all enemies foreign and domestic…to bear true faith and allegiance to the same."[35] This statement implies actions within and/or beyond our borders against any individual(s) regardless of citizenship, that present a threat to the nation. Maintaining "true faith and allegiance" to the principles guiding the nation make any action contrary to our law an inherent violation of this oath. This is an understanding all military officers must possess in the execution their duties. During the Senate debate regarding the Homeland Security Act Senator Byrd eloquently cautioned:

> "We have a responsibility to ourselves and to future generations to ensure that, in our zeal to build a fortress against terrorism, we are not dismantling the fortress of our organic law--our Constitution--our liberties, and our American way of life."[36]

---

[35] U. S. Code Title 5, Section 3331, (1966).
[36] Congress. Senate. Congressional Record "Debate on Homeland Security Act of 2002." (17 Sept 2002), S8649.

Bibliography

Baker, Bonnie. "The Origins of the Posse Comitatus." Aerospace Power Chronicles (November 1999).

Benson, Nolon J. The Posse Comitatus Act: Is there a need for Change?, Carlisle Barrack, PA: U.S. Army War College, 1998.

Dao, James. "Cheney Supports Domestic Antiterrorism Military Command." New York Times, 28 January 2002, A7:3.

Doyle, Charles. The Posse Comitatus Act & Related Matters: The Use of the Military to Execute Civilian Law. Washington, DC: Library of Congress. Congressional Research Service, 1995.

Dunlap, Charles J., Jr. "The Origins of the American Military Coup of 2012." Parameters 22, no.4 (Winter 1992/1993): 2-20.

Elliot Scott. "Eberhart Briefs Congress on U.S. Northern Command." 14 March 2002. <www.northcom.mil>, [28 March 2003].

Engdahl, David E. "Foundations for the Military Intervention in the United States." In Military Intervention in Democratic Societies, ed. Peter J. Rowe and Christopher J. Whelan, 1-50. London: Croom Helm, 1985.

Gentner, Judith L. "The American Dilemma: Freedoms or Security." U.S. Army War College, Carlisle Barracks, PA: 1999.

Grove, Gregory D. The U.S. Military and the Civil Infrastructure Protection: Restrictions and Discretion under the Posse Comitatus Act. Stanford, CA: Center for International Security and Cooperation, 1999.

Haskell, Bob. "New Security Department Reinforces NORTHCOM Mission." 26 Nov 2002 <http://www.pentagon.mil/news/Nov2002/n11262002_200211262.html>, [14 March 2003].

McCullough, David. John Adams. Simon & Schuster, 2001.

Public Law 107-56, "USA Patriot Act," 26 Oct 2001.

Public Law 107-296, "Homeland Security Act of 2002," 25 Nov 2002.

Schlichter, Kurt Andrew, Locked and Loaded: Taking Aim at the Growing Use of the American Military in Civilian Law Enforcement Operations, Loyola of Los Angeles Law Review, Summer 1993. News/Wires. Lexis-Nexis. Los Angeles, CA: Lexis-Nexis. (4 April 2003).

Sonnenblick, Mark. Will USNORTHCOM Bring Us Military Dictatorship After Oct 1? Executive Intelligence Weekly, 19 May 2002.

United States Code. Title 5, Section 3331. (1966).

United States Code. Title 10, Sections 371-382. (1981).

United States Code. Title 18, Section 831. (1982).

United States Code. Title 18, Section 1365. (1956).

U.S. Congress. Senate. "Homeland Security Act of 2002." Congressional Record. Page S8644-S8649, 17 Sept 2002.

U.S. Department of Defense. Unified Command Plan. Washington, DC: April 2002.

Office of Homeland Security. National Strategy for Homeland Security. Washington, DC: July 2002.

U.S. Department of Homeland Security. The National Security Strategy ot the United States of America. Washington, DC: September 2002.

U.S. Department of Homeland Security. National Strategy to Combat Weapons of Mass Destruction. Washington, DC: December 2002.

U.S. Department of Navy, Military Personnel Manual, NAVPERS 15560D. 22 August 2002.

U.S. President. Presidential Decision Directive 63. "Critical Infrastructure Protection." 22 May 1998.